DISASTERS

EARTHQUAKES

ANN WEIL

SADDLEBACK
EDUCATIONAL PUBLISHING

DISASTERS

SADDLEBACK
EDUCATIONAL PUBLISHING
www.sdlback.com

Copyright © 2004, 2013 by Saddleback Educational Publishing
All rights reserved. No part of this book may be reproduced in any form or by any means, electronic or mechanical, including photocopying, recording, scanning, or by any information storage and retrieval system, without the written permission of the publisher. SADDLEBACK EDUCATIONAL PUBLISHING and any associated logos are trademarks and/or registered trademarks of Saddleback Educational Publishing.

ISBN-13: 978-1-61651-929-2
ISBN-10: 1-61651-929-0
eBook: 978-61247-625-4

Printed in Guangzhou, China
0712/CA21201056

17 16 15 14 13   1 2 3 4 5

Photo Credits: page 29, Richard Berenholtz/Corbis; page 37, Owen Franken/Corbis; page 61, Bettemann/Corbis; page 70, © David Snyder | Dreamstime.com; page 81, © Arindam Banerjee | Dreamstime.com; page 89, The Asahi Shimbun / The Asahi Shimbun / Getty Images

CONTENTS

DATAFILE

Timeline

1811, 1812

Earthquakes cause the Mississippi River to flow upstream.

1935

Charles Richter invents the Richter Scale to measure the power of earthquakes.

Where is the Pacific Ring of Fire?

HERE

Key Terms

Pacific Ring of Fire—a band around the Pacific Ocean where two tectonic plates (part of the Earth's crust) meet

Richter Scale—a scale used to measure the strength of earthquakes

shock waves—energy that travels underground, but causes earthquakes at the surface

tsunami—huge waves created by an earthquake or volcano underwater

CHAPTER 1 | Introduction

You hear a rumbling louder than thunder. The ground begins to shake. It's an earthquake!

Earthquakes can be deadly. Many last a minute or less. But in those few seconds entire cities can crumble. Buildings and bridges collapse. People are crushed or buried alive.

Millions have died in earthquakes. Even after an earthquake stops, the damage may continue. Fires break out. These fires can destroy even more than the earthquake itself.

Some earthquakes happen underwater. These can cause big ocean waves called tsunami.

Tsunami are huge walls of water. They crash down on land with tremendous force. Tsunami caused by earthquakes kill many thousands of people all over the world.

Tsunami are giant waves that hit the shore. Some are as tall as a ten-story building. Tsunami are not very big when they are out at sea. But, out in the ocean, they travel faster than a speeding bullet.

Near land, they suck up all the water near the shore. Then they crash down. They can smash and wash away buildings. People are crushed and swept out to sea.

Why Do Earthquakes Happen?

The top layer of our planet is called the crust. It seems solid to us. In fact it's broken into giant pieces. These pieces are called tectonic plates.

Plates are always moving. They move very slowly. Sometimes plates slide past each other. Sometimes they push against each other. In some places, plates pull away from each other.

All this movement creates pressure underground. The pressure builds up. It causes huge chunks of rock to break. It's as if a bomb has exploded underground.

An enormous amount of energy is released. Some of this energy is in the form of shock waves. Shock waves travel through the ground. Some of them reach the surface. When they do, they can cause tremendous damage.

Severe earthquakes can lift huge stones off the ground. The ground can shake so much that buildings tumble down like a house of cards.

Highways crack open. Cars may be swallowed up. It's impossible to stand or run during a bad earthquake. People become helpless. Earthquakes are one of our deadliest natural disasters.

The Pacific Ring of Fire

Most earthquakes happen near where two plates meet. Most of the world's earthquakes occur in a band around the Pacific Ocean. This band is called the Pacific Ring of Fire.

Parts of California are on the Pacific Ring of Fire. So is Japan. There are many cities along the Pacific Ring of Fire. When an earthquake hits a big city, it can be a disaster.

Measuring Earthquakes

There are millions of earthquakes each year. Most of these are very mild. Only about 100,000 can be felt. Fortunately, only a small fraction of earthquakes cause disasters. Only about 100 cause any damage at all.

There are different ways to measure earthquakes. Scientists use a machine called a seismograph to detect earthquakes. It also measures and records the strength of earthquakes.

The Richter Scale is based on these measurements. Charles Richter developed the Richter Scale in the 1930s.

It is the most commonly used scale to rank and measure earthquakes.

The Richter Scale goes from 0 to 9. Serious earthquakes usually measure more than 7.0 on the Richter Scale. Earthquakes less than 5.0 rarely cause any damage.

Each number on the scale represents ten times the power of the previous one. So, an earthquake that measures 8.0 on the Richter Scale is ten times more powerful than one that measures 7.0.

Another way to measure earthquakes is to ask people what they felt and saw during an earthquake. The Mercalli Scale is based on what people see and say. It describes how much damage an earthquake causes.

The Mercalli Scale:

1. Most people don't feel the earthquake.

2. A few people notice shaking.

3. People indoors think a truck has passed by outside. Hanging objects may swing. People may not realize that it is an earthquake.

4. Windows, dishes, and glasses rattle. People inside may feel a jolt as if something has hit the house. Parked cars rock.

5. Doors swing open and shut. Buildings shake. Liquid slops out of glasses.

6. Everyone feels it. Plaster cracks. Things fall off shelves. Windows break. Trees sway.

7. People can't stand up. Loose bricks and tiles tumble down.

8. Chimneys fall down. Cracks open in the ground.

9. People panic. Some buildings collapse.

10. Many buildings collapse.

11. The ground cracks open. Train tracks bend and break.

12. All buildings are destroyed. The landscape is totally changed.

Earthquake Oddities

An earthquake once made the Mississippi River flow backwards! In 1811 and 1812, there were tremendous earthquakes in the southern states. Water in the great Mississippi River flowed upstream for a short amount of time.

The water flooded forests. It created new lakes. You can still see some of these lakes today. Earthquakes created Reelfoot Lake in Tennessee.

Earthquakes even happen on the moon. But there are not as many as on Earth. And moon-quakes are less severe. They occur about halfway between the surface and the center of the moon.

The moon

DATAFILE

Timeline

April 18, 1906

The Great Earthquake strikes San Francisco a little after 5 a.m.

October 17, 1989

An earthquake strikes San Francisco. It lasts for 15 seconds.

Where is San Francisco?

HERE

Key Terms

fault—a place where two plates scrape against each other

rubble—broken pieces of a building

aftershocks—smaller earthquakes after the main one

San Francisco is a city with a lot of history. In the 1700s, Spanish people came from Mexico. They built a fort there in 1776. It is called the Presidio.

The Spanish also built a mission. They named the mission after Saint Francis. They called it San Francisco de Asis. That's how San Francisco got its name.

The Gold Rush

California joined the United States in 1846. There were fewer than a thousand people living there then. Then some people found gold in California. Thousands rushed to California. They hoped to find gold, too. This was the start of the Gold Rush.

San Francisco quickly grew to 20,000 people. The Gold Rush ended. But people still came. San Francisco bay filled with ships.

By 1906, almost half a million people lived there. It was the largest city west of the Missouri River.

There were always earthquakes in San Francisco. People who lived there felt small ones every year. And there were strong ones in 1839, 1865, 1868, 1892, and 1898.

Everyone knew about the earthquakes. But they didn't understand why the ground under their city shook so much.

San Andreas Fault

San Francisco is built over a place where two plates meet. The Pacific and North American plates rub and scrape against each other. The strain of this has created the San Andreas Fault.

The San Andreas Fault is more than 800 miles long. In some places, you can even see it from the air. It looks like a big, long crack in the ground.

There are also many smaller faults in the area. Some connect to the main fault. Others spread out. This area is one of the weakest parts of the Earth's crust.

There are many earthquakes around the San Andreas Fault. Scientists record about 20,000 tremors every year. Not all cause damage. Most are mild. They don't last very long.

But some are very powerful. Some are strong enough to shake buildings until they break up.

These are the earthquakes people fear. And this is the sort of earthquake that struck San Francisco in 1906.

The Great Earthquake

The Great Earthquake of 1906 began just past 5:00 a.m. Most were still in bed. A loud rumble woke people up.

Buildings swung from side to side. Furniture tipped over and broke. People were thrown out of bed. Bricks fell from buildings. Windows shattered.

People were terrified. They felt helpless. There was nothing they could do.

Chimneys crumbled. There were terrifying crashes as buildings collapsed floor by floor. People were crushed under the rubble.

The first tremor was the worst. It went on for about one minute. When buildings shook apart, the people inside were crushed. Many died instantly. Others were trapped under the rubble.

Water gushed from burst pipes. It flooded many buildings. The trapped survivors could not escape. Many people drowned.

There were also strong aftershocks. Aftershocks happen after an earthquake. The ground shakes again as it settles back down.

Already damaged buildings gave way to the aftershocks. Metal trolley tracks twisted up like pretzels. The waterfront was a wreck. Survivors were in shock. But worse was still to come.

Fire!

The earthquake knocked over ovens. It broke gas pipes. There were many gas leaks. Fires broke out all over the city. Gas leaks fueled the flames.

There was no water to fight the fires. The earthquake had broken all the water pipes.

People trapped in the ruined buildings burned to death. Eighty people died that way in one hotel.

Fires burned for days. These fires destroyed more than the earthquake itself. Buildings that had survived the earthquake were gutted by fire.

The army was called in. They used dynamite to blow up whole streets. They were trying to stop the fire from spreading. Soldiers also shot anyone caught stealing. Many people were killed for looting.

Finally, the last fire burned itself out. Most of the city was destroyed.

More than half the city's people were homeless. Most camped out at Golden Gate Park. Others went to the old Spanish Presidio.

Some people thought everyone should leave the city. Why rebuild when another earthquake could happen at any time?

But San Francisco was rebuilt. It now has twice as many people as it did a hundred years ago. And it still has earthquakes.

October 17, 1989

The 1906 earthquake measured 8.3 on the Richter Scale. That's an enormous earthquake. But even a smaller earthquake can cause a tremendous amount of damage. This is especially true when it hits a busy city like modern-day San Francisco.

The earthquake that struck San Francisco on October 17, 1989 measured 7.1 on the Richter Scale. That's less than one-tenth as powerful as the 1906 earthquake.

The 1989 earthquake lasted only fifteen seconds. But it caused an elevated highway to collapse. Huge chunks of concrete fell onto cars below. Forty-two people died.

The 1989 earthquake caused at least $6 billion worth of damage. Many of the city's old wooden buildings collapsed. 12,000 people became homeless. The San Andreas Fault had struck again.

The Next Big One?

The San Andreas Fault runs almost the entire length of California. Millions of people live in places at high risk for earthquakes. We can't stop earthquakes. But we can work to lessen their damage.

Modern office buildings in California are built to withstand tremors. They can stay standing even during a big earthquake. Children practice earthquake drills in school. They learn what to do when there is an earthquake.

Scientists watch the San Andreas Fault. They try to predict when and where the next big earthquake will hit. They use laser beams to watch the plates for movement.

Sometimes there are changes in underground water before an earthquake. These changes result from shifting rocks. So scientists check water levels in wells. They also look for unusual minerals and gases in the water.

But even so, predicting earthquakes is very difficult. It's still a mystery when and where the next big one will hit.

California Earthquake Facts

The earliest reported earthquake in California was in 1769. It was felt by a group of explorers. They were camping about 30 miles from Los Angeles.

The San Andreas Fault is always moving. But it moves very slowly. It moves about two inches a year. This is about the same rate at which your fingernails grow.

The Transamerica Pyramid office building in San Francisco was designed to survive a major earthquake.

DATAFILE

Timeline

1521

Spanish soldiers destroy the Mexican city
Tenochtitlán.

September 19, 1985

An earthquake shakes Mexico City. The shock
waves are stronger than an atomic bomb.

Where is Mexico City?

HERE

Did You Know?

When the earthquake hit Mexico City, a hospital collapsed. Babies were rescued after a week of being buried in the rubble!

Key Terms

Tenochtitlán—possibly the largest city in the fourteenth-century world; built on islands in Lake Texcoco, Mexico

lake bed—the ground at the bottom of a lake

CHAPTER 3 | Mexico City, 1985

Mexico is in North America. It was once part of the Aztec Empire. The Aztecs were Native Americans. Around 1325, the Aztecs built a city on an island in Lake Texcoco.

They called it Tenochtitlán. Tenochtitlán became a city of islands. The Aztecs used boats to travel from one part of the city to another.

Tenochtitlán was the capital of the Aztec Empire. The Aztecs ruled much of Mexico for about two hundred years.

Tenochtitlán was perhaps the largest city in the world. It had a huge temple complex. There was also a royal palace.

Spanish soldiers invaded in 1521. They conquered the Aztecs. They destroyed Tenochtitlán. The Spanish built Mexico City on the ruins of the old Aztec city.

Lake Texcoco dried up. Mexico City spread out over the dry lake bed. More and more people came to live there. By 1985, it was a huge city. About 18 million people lived and worked there.

The lake bed under Mexico City is mostly mud and clay. It is very soft. Soft ground shakes more than hard rock during an earthquake. This means more earthquake damage to buildings built on soft ground.

The Earthquake

On September 19, 1985, there was a massive earthquake. There were two jolts.

Rocks slipped along a 124-mile fault. This happened about 12 miles below the surface.

The earthquake released tremendous shock waves. These shock waves were more powerful than an atomic bomb. The earthquake measured 8.1 on the Richter Scale.

More than 400 buildings in Mexico City collapsed within five minutes of the first tremor. 3,000 more were badly damaged. Some of these were large high-rise apartments.

More than 30,000 people were badly hurt. At least 100,000 people lost their homes. Reports said that 10,000 people died. But the exact number may never be known.

The Search for Survivors

After the earthquake, rescue workers searched the wreckage. Survivors were trapped for days in collapsed buildings.

Some rescue equipment can sense body heat. That tells the rescuers where to look. But this equipment is costly. It can be hard to get.

The Mexicans did not have a lot of basic rescue equipment. There weren't enough cranes. There weren't enough saws to cut through concrete. They couldn't move the rubble safely.

Rescue workers sometimes die trying to save others. It is very dangerous work. Still they managed to pull many people out alive. They rescued families from the apartment buildings. But many more died because they could not be rescued in time.

Amazing Survival Stories

One of the buildings that collapsed was a hospital. The top floors fell onto the ones below. Many patients were crushed to death.

There were many newborn babies in the hospital nursery. Many of these babies survived after being buried for seven days. More than 50 infants were rescued alive.

The highest office building in Mexico survived. All 52 floors are still standing. It survived the shock waves of the 1985 earthquake.

Rescue workers pull a body out from the rubble of a build-ing destroyed by an earthquake in Mexico City.

DATAFILE

Timeline

September 1, 1923

More than 100,000 people die when an earthquake hits Tokyo, Japan.

January 17, 1995

An earthquake measuring 7.2 on the Richter Scale strikes Kobe, Japan.

Where is Tokyo?

HERE

Did You Know?

After the 1923 earthquake, a woman saved herself and her baby from the ensuing fires by standing in the water all day.

Key Terms

epicenter—the ground above where the earthquake starts

scorch—to burn

CHAPTER 4 | Japan, 1923 & 1995

Japan is a country of islands. These islands are on the Pacific Ring of Fire. There are many active volcanoes in Japan.

Japan also has lots of earthquakes. Most are mild. But some are very deadly.

Tokyo, September 1, 1923

Tokyo is the capital city of Japan. It is located on Honshu, Japan's largest island.

In 1923, Tokyo was the fifth largest city in the world. More than 2.5 million people lived there.

That year, a violent earthquake shook most of Honshu. The earthquake measured 8.3 on the Richter Scale.

The shaking was very intense. It registered as high as 12 on the Mercalli Scale. That's the highest possible rating.

Thousands of homes in Tokyo crumpled instantly. Roofs caved in on people. Cooking stoves were smashed. Fires broke out.

The Tokyo fires were much worse than the ones in San Francisco after the 1906 earthquake. The fires grew and spread quickly. Thousands who survived the earthquake were burned to death.

People tried to escape the blaze. Many ran to parks. They hoped the fire wouldn't follow them there.

Some people stood up to their necks in water. One woman saved herself and her baby this way. She stood in the water all day holding her baby on top of her head.

Others were not so lucky. Flames blew over the water. The fire scorched their heads and they died. But under the water, their bodies were untouched.

Tokyo was not the only city affected by the earthquake. The port city of Yokohama was also destroyed.

Fires broke out in Yokohama, too. People ran to the sea. But many oil tanks had burst. Burning oil covered the surface of the water.

The earthquake also caused a tsunami. Altogether, about 143,000 people died. 100,000 were in Tokyo. Fires killed about half the people.

Half a million homes were destroyed. The earthquake and fire made more than a million people homeless overnight.

Some parents lost their children. Children became orphans. People searched for days for lost relatives.

The fiery-hot air burned people's throats. They could not speak. Instead they held out pieces of paper with their names written out.

Finally, the fires ended. People searched the ashes of their homes for lost possessions. But the fire left very little for them to find.

Japan Earthquake Facts

September 1st is Disaster Prevention Day in Tokyo. Special memorial services are held in honor of the victims of the 1923 earthquake.

The 1923 earthquake also caused massive landslides in the nearby mountains.

The 1923 earthquake was actually underneath the water. The epicenter was in Sagami Bay, which is about 50 miles from Tokyo.

Kobe, 1995

A sudden and severe earthquake shook Honshu again on January 17, 1995. This time the earthquake was centered near the south of the island. The industrial port city of Kobe was hardest hit.

The 1995 earthquake measured 7.2 on the Richter Scale. It shook the city of Kobe for 20 seconds.

Broken gas pipes burst into flames all over the city. Water pipes burst.

About 5,500 people were killed. 100,000 buildings were destroyed.

Many of the newer buildings survived. They had been built with earthquakes in mind.

CHAPTER 5 | Lisbon, 1755

DATAFILE

Timeline

1754

The French and Indian War begins.

November 1, 1755

Lisbon, Portugal, is destroyed by an earthquake,
followed by fires and tsunami.

Where is Lisbon?

HERE

Key Terms

harbor—a place where boats dock to be safe from storms

priceless—too valuable to have a price

capsize—to overturn

CHAPTER 5 | Lisbon, 1755

Lisbon became the capital city of Portugal in 1256. It was the main port city for the Portuguese Empire. By 1755, it was home to more than a quarter of a million people.

Lisbon was one of the largest and most beautiful cities in Europe. It had a busy harbor on the Tagus River. There were castles, churches, and a grand cathedral.

The Earthquake

On November 1, 1755, a powerful earthquake hit Lisbon. It was a holiday. Many people were in the city's churches. They were lighting candles for All Saints Day.

At 9:40 a.m., there was a loud rumble. People were frightened. They ran outside. But what they saw was even more terrifying.

The earthquake was pushing the ground up into the air. People couldn't stand or walk. Everyone panicked. But there was nothing they could do.

Buildings collapsed all over the city. Thousands were killed instantly. Many survivors rushed toward the river. Some jumped onto ships. They hoped to escape.

Others gathered on the new stone pier that ran along the river's edge. They thought they would be safe there. But they were wrong.

Tsunami

Three tsunami traveled from the Atlantic Ocean to the Tagus River. They crashed into Lisbon Harbor. The people on the pier were washed away. Boats capsized. Many drowned.

Fire

Still, the disaster continued. Hundreds of fires burned in the city. Some were started by overturned candles. Others were caused by cooking stoves and lamps.

Fires burned for days. When the smoke finally cleared, the city was a complete ruin. More than 60,000 people had died.

City in Ruins

The fire and earthquake destroyed most of Lisbon. The tsunami wrecked the waterfront. More than half the city's churches were totally ruined. The rest were badly damaged. Many priceless works of art were also destroyed.

Many survivors left the city. Their experience was too awful for them to stay.

The Richter Scale had not yet been invented. Scientists estimate that the Lisbon earthquake was about 8.7 on the Richter Scale.

DATAFILE

Timeline

1831 BCE

Earliest recorded earthquake occurs.

July 28, 1976

The deadliest earthquake of the twentieth century hits Tangshan, China.

Where is Tangshan?

Key Terms

BCE—before the Common Era, replaces previously used BC (before Christ), which covers the period of history before Christ was born

eyewitness—a person who sees something happen

rupture—to burst or break

CHAPTER 6 | China

China has a long history of earthquakes. Some of the deadliest earthquakes ever have happened in China.

We don't know a lot about ancient earthquakes. Back then, only a few people then had a written language. This means there are very few records of ancient earthquakes.

The Chinese had a written language long before most others. They wrote down many things. They also recorded earthquakes. Many of these records were lost. But some survived.

The earliest recorded earthquake happened in China. It was in 1831 BCE. That's almost four thousand years ago!

Key Dates

1831 BCE: The earliest recorded earthquake in the world happens in China.

780 BCE: The Chinese began a complete record of Chinese earthquakes.

1556: More than 800,000 people die in an earthquake.

1920: An earthquake starts a landslide. 200,000 people die.

1927: An earthquake that measures 8.3 on the Richter Scale kills about 200,000 people.

1976: An earthquake hits near Tangshan. Reports from China say that 255,000 people died. But some say more than twice that number died.

There are no other records of Chinese earthquakes that happened long ago. But there are more complete records of earthquakes starting in 780 BCE.

The world's deadliest recorded earthquake happened in 1556. It struck in central China.

Most people there lived in caves. They carved their homes out of soft rock. The caves collapsed during the earthquake. About 830,000 people were killed.

Preventing Disaster

We can't stop earthquakes. But we can sometimes predict them. Scientists know several warning signs that an earthquake is about to happen.

One of these is a change in underground water levels. Sometimes rocks move around just before an earthquake. This causes water underground to move, too.

In early February 1975, a radio broadcast warned the residents of Haicheng to leave immediately. Scientists had noticed that water levels in wells were changing. Then there were small tremors.

On February 4 there was a powerful earthquake. It measured 7.5 on the Richter Scale. Thousands of buildings collapsed. Some people died. But it could have been much deadlier without the warning.

A successful earthquake prediction is a great achievement. It can save thousands of lives. But scientists can't predict every earthquake.

China suffered another powerful earthquake a year later. This time there was no warning. It came as a surprise, a very deadly surprise.

1976, Tangshan

On July 28, 1976, an earthquake struck the city of Tangshan. The earthquake happened in the middle of the night. Almost everyone was asleep.

Eyewitnesses saw a bright flash across the sky. That was followed by a deafening roar. Then the shaking began.

Roofs caved in. Some concrete buildings collapsed. The top floors fell onto the ones below. Many people were crushed to death without even waking up.

It was almost impossible to rescue people in the dark. The earthquake had knocked out the power. There were no lights. It was pitch-black outside. Many people died before they could be saved.

The earthquake measured 8.2 on the Richter Scale. It happened along a 150-km (93-mile) fault. The entire fault ruptured. That released a huge amount of energy. Powerful shock waves rippled out underground.

This massive earthquake may have triggered a second one. There was an aftershock about 16 hours later. It struck the same area. This second earthquake measured at least 7.6 on the Richter Scale.

Many of Tangshan's newer buildings survived the first earthquake. But the second earthquake did even more damage than the first. Everything was flattened. The city was totally destroyed. No buildings were left standing.

Some workers were trapped in nearby coal mines. They were stuck under ground for hours or days. But many of them were finally rescued.

The Chinese government said that more than 600,000 people were badly hurt, and about a quarter million died. More recent studies say that closer to half a million died. Either way, this was the deadliest quake in the twentieth century.

Damaged buildings in a popular shopping district near Beijing after the 1976 earthquake in Tangshan.

DATAFILE

Timeline

July 9, 1958

An 8.2 magnitude earthquake in the Gulf of Alaska triggers a tsunami with waves over 1,720 feet high. These are the highest ever recorded.

December 26, 2004

A massive earthquake-triggered tsunami devastates eleven coastal countries around the Indian Ocean.

Where is the Indian Ocean?

HERE

Key Terms

epicenter—the part of the Earth's surface directly above the focus of an earthquake

impact—to have a direct effect on

jetty, jetties—a structure extended into the sea to protect a harbor

CHAPTER 9 | Tsunami, 2004

The Indian Ocean is the third-largest ocean after the Pacific and Atlantic. It stretches for more than 6,000 miles between Africa and Australia.

The Indian Ocean is very important to the world's economy. Two thirds of the world's oil shipments use waterways in the Indian Ocean. Some of these waterways are legendary, such as the Suez Canal and the Strait of Hormuz. Half of the world's cargo ships pass through the Indian Ocean every year.

People around the world depend on the Indian Ocean. One third of the Earth's population lives in countries that have a coastline on the Indian Ocean. A natural disaster in this part of the world would have a devastating human and economic impact.

The Earthquake and Tsunami 2004

On December 26, 2004, at 7:58 p.m. local time, a magnitude 9.0 earthquake struck off the coast of the Indonesian island of Sumatra. Hundreds of miles of seafloor was ripped apart. Powerful shockwaves blasted in all directions. Eleven countries on the coast of the Indian Ocean were about to be devastated.

In coastal cities, the waves seemed to come from nowhere. Witnesses on the beaches said that the ocean first retreated. There was an eerie few moments of silence. Then they heard a faint roaring sound. In the distance, they could see white caps on the tops of the waves. Then the water poured over the beaches. Waves were as high as 30 feet.

Within hours, survivors picked through their villages looking for loved ones. The hospitals and morgues were overwhelmed. Several hospitals that were still standing announced they had run out of body bags. In several of the affected countries, the dead were buried in mass graves.

The Deadliest Tsunami in History

More than 230,000 people died in the quake and resulting tsunami. Two million people were displaced from their homes. Scientists believe that this was the most powerful earthquake to hit South Asia in more than 40 years.

Indonesia, Sri Lanka, and India were the countries hardest hit by the earthquake and tsunami. Other countries that suffered damage and loss of life include Thailand, Malaysia, Burma, Bangladesh, Somalia, Kenya, Tanzania, and the Seychelles.

Indonesia

Indonesia suffered the most damage and loss of life. This was because it was so close to the epicenter of the earthquake. There was little time to escape the rushing waves. The tsunami hit less than a half hour after the earthquake happened.

Survivors were overwhelmed by huge, black, soupy waves of water shooting through the streets. Cars and homes smashed into buildings and crushed men, women, and children. Survivors hung from railings, reaching for neighbors and loved ones. Some were pulled to safety. Others were swept into foaming waves full of twisted metal and wood.

Particularly hard-hit were the provinces of Aceh and North Sumatra. More than 170,000 died in these areas. The important fishing industry was destroyed. Nearly 45 percent of the residents lost their livelihoods. A year later, 60,000 people were still living in tents.

Sri Lanka

In Sri Lanka, more than 100,000 homes were destroyed. Fishing boats were smashed. More than 30,000 died and 4,000 were missing and presumed dead. Land mines planted during a long civil war washed into unknown parts of the country.

India

India's southeast coast was flooded as the tsunami rushed as far as two miles inland. More than 15,000 homes were destroyed. Three hundred miles of roads and many bridges were damaged. This delayed help for survivors. India's mainland suffered at least 9,000 casualties.

India's Andaman and Nicobar Islands also suffered heavy destruction. Salt water from the tsunami contaminated many wells and thousands of acres of farmland. Jetties used to get supplies to the islanders were wrecked. This contributed to survivors not getting timely assistance.

Thailand

Many tourist areas in Thailand, like Phuket, were destroyed. Thousands of foreign tourists were killed. Much of the video footage of the disaster was captured by tourists. They recorded images of waves crashing over their hotels before they fled for their lives.

Years Later

Years later, not all of the devastated countries have been rebuilt. Across the region, the fishing industry lost approximately $520 million. Fishermen still struggle to make a living. There are still 70,000 people in government shelters, and another 20,000 still in tents in Aceh Province alone. Doctors worry about victims contacting mosquito-borne diseases like dengue fever and malaria. These diseases happen when pools of water are left by a tsunami. The

More than 1,500 people were killed when this passenger-packed train was struck by the tsunami in Galle, Sri Lanka. Here it has just been placed back on the tracks.

problem was made worse by the destruction of thousands of wells and sanitation facilities.

What Could Have Been Done?

An effective early warning system might have saved lives. These systems use scientific devices tethered to the sea bottom. They record data that includes wave activity. If there are dangerous readings, information is relayed to authorities. Often the information does not get to the people who are in danger. These people are poor. They do not have access to phones or computers.

There is an effort underway to get warning systems in place around the world as soon as possible before the next earthquake or tsunami hits.

DATAFILE

Timeline

January 12, 2010

In the late afternoon, an earthquake measuring 7.0 on the Richter Scale hits the small island nation of Haiti.

October 2010

A cholera outbreak further devastates a still recovering Haiti.

Where is Haiti?

Did You Know?

Haiti occupies the western third of the island of Hispaniola. It is the poorest country in the Americas with a population of 9.8 million people.

Key Terms

contaminated—make (something) impure by exposure to or addition of a poisonous or polluting substance

poverty—the state of being extremely poor

sanitation—conditions relating to public health, such as providing clean drinking water or adequate sewage disposal

The Republic of Haiti is on the island of Hispaniola, which it shares with the Dominican Republic. Hispaniola was discovered by Christopher Columbus in 1492. Haiti gets its name from the indigenous Taíno or Amerindian word "ayiti" which means "land of high mountains."

Agriculture is a major part of the economy in Haiti. Sugar, coffee, mangoes, cocoa, and sugarcane are important crops. So why is Haiti the poorest country in the Western Hemisphere?

One reason is that Haiti is fast becoming a desert because most of the trees have been cut down. The treeless land is of poor quality for farming. Many rural farmers are forced to travel to the capital of Port-au-Prince for work. But there are few jobs available. Haiti's extreme poverty means there is little money to construct roads and buildings up to international safety standards. This makes Haiti especially vulnerable to natural disasters.

The Earthquake

On Tuesday, January 12, 2010, at 4:53 p.m. local time, a powerful earthquake measuring 7.0 on the Richter Scale hit Haiti. The quake was centered just 15 miles southwest of the capital of Port-au-Prince. For almost a minute, tremors shook buildings and terrified Port-au-Prince's nearly two million residents. It had been 200 years since Haiti suffered an earthquake of this magnitude.

The Haiti earthquake happened on a fault line that runs along the boundary between the Caribbean and North American plates. These rocky plates normally fit together like a giant jigsaw puzzle. But when they slip against each other, tremendous energy is released underground. Geologists say this fault line resembles the San Andreas Fault in California.

Since the Haiti earthquake was centered on the major population center of Port-au-Prince, casualties were high. The Haitian government estimates that more than 300,000 people died. Many were trapped in poorly constructed homes and office buildings. As many as 60,000 of these buildings were damaged or destroyed.

After the first shock wave passed, survivors stumbled about the city looking for help. Many were injured and bleeding. Some held crying children. Clouds of thick, white dust from the rubble covered people's faces and clothing. Haiti's National Cathedral and Presidential Palace collapsed. Even the president of Haiti had nowhere to go.

Rescue crews struggled to get to survivors. Roads were blocked by rocks, downed trees, and crushed vehicles. Injured survivors who made it to hospitals found them destroyed. Medical personnel tried to bring the injured to local schools. Most of them were also in ruins.

Other nations reached out to help Haiti. But they were initially unable to safely fly in food, water, and medicines. The control tower at the Port-au-Prince airport was damaged. Despite the danger, planes were eventually able to make their way to Haiti with aid for the victims.

With buildings destroyed and no shelters available, tent cities were created on streets, parks, and even golf courses. Many of these structures had only plastic sheets for walls and roofs. Thousands of people were forced to bathe in the streets. They used plastic buckets and contaminated water.

The Recovery

Haiti's recovery was complicated by the destruction of most public buildings in Port-au-Prince. Many of Haiti's most experienced government officials were killed or injured in the earthquake. These officials could have helped the country deal more effectively with the crisis.

Most survivors in Haiti showed great courage in the aftermath of the earthquake. They dug with their hands to rescue those trapped inside flattened buildings. Others showed a more sinister side of human behavior. Shortages of food and water caused some to steal from shops. As soon as relief supplies started to arrive in Port-au-Prince, the looting mostly stopped.

A Bad Situation Becomes Worse

Two incidents turned the 2010 Haiti earthquake into an even greater tragedy. The first was a major 6.0 aftershock on January 20. Many damaged buildings that were still standing crumpled to the ground.

The second incident happened about nine months later. The initial January 12 earthquake had damaged water and sanitation systems. Most of these had not been repaired. People were reduced to drinking water that was also used for bathing. These were the perfect conditions for a cholera outbreak.

Cholera is a bacterial disease that results primarily from lack of clean water and sanitation. Symptoms of cholera include severe diarrhea and vomiting. If patients are not given liquids quickly, they become dehydrated. Dehydration can lead to shock and even death. The young and old are especially vulnerable. Haitian officials estimate that more than 500,000 people contracted cholera in the two years after the earthquake.

Rebuilding Port-au-Prince and the rest of Haiti could take decades. Many of the damaged schools have not been rebuilt. Two years later, more than 500,000 earthquake survivors still live in settlement camps. Most of Port-au-Prince is still in ruins. A combined effort is needed. The Haitian people and their government must work together to rebuild Haiti.

Life goes on in Port-au-Prince, Haiti, where most of the downtown buildings remain untouched and dangerous.

DATAFILE

Timeline

March 11, 2011

A 9.0 magnitude earthquake occurs eighty miles off the central coast of Honshu, the main island of Japan.

March 11, 2011

The quake triggers a massive tsunami less than an hour later.

Where is Japan?

HERE

Key Terms

aftershock—a tremor (or one of a series of tremors) occurring after the main shock of an earthquake

magnitude—measure of the energy released during an earthquake; the great size or extent of something

tremor—a small earthquake

CHAPTER 9 | Japan, 2011

On March 11, 2011, Honshu, the main island of Japan, was again the scene of a devastating earthquake. At 2:46 p.m. local time, the first tremors hit in the ocean 80 miles east of the central coast of Sendai City in the Miyagi Prefecture. The Pacific Ring of Fire was generating a monster earthquake measuring 9.0 on the Richter Scale. This would be the largest earthquake to ever hit Japan and one of the five worst earthquakes ever recorded.

In seconds, a tragically familiar scene unfolded. The initial tremors began without warning. According to witnesses, the ground trembled for nearly five minutes. Buildings shook. Windows shattered, raining glass down onto the street. Inside homes, walls collapsed, sending people and possessions flying. Stairwells twisted and narrowed, cutting off escape routes for many people inside. Even 230 miles away in Tokyo, buildings shook violently.

On the streets, pavement buckled, crushing cars and trucks. Roads were impassible. Oil refineries burst into flames and shot toxic black clouds into the air. Modern office and residential buildings had been built to withstand earthquakes, and they survived by swaying like trees in the wind. Sadly, thousands of other buildings not built to current construction standards were destroyed.

The initial quake was quickly followed by at least five serious aftershocks. Some of these aftershocks registered as high as 7.0 on the Richter Scale. This qualified these aftershocks as major earthquakes. Approximately 50 aftershocks hit the first day, each threatening more devastation. According to experts, it is the uncertainty and fear of aftershocks that causes much of the stress for earthquake survivors.

A chain of horrible events continued to unravel. Less than an hour after the initial tremors hit, walls of water, some more than 30 feet high, crashed over Honshu. Churning waves of water crushed cars, buses, and boats and tossed them around like toys in a bathtub. Swirling whirlpools tore through streets, destroying houses and businesses. Many people were swept up in the water and washed out to sea.

Terrified residents ran for higher ground, often climbing onto trees or the roofs of buildings. But the eastern shore of Honshu Island is mostly flat. This prevented many people from finding higher ground to escape to.

And then the unthinkable happened. The power of the quake and resulting tsunami damaged the cooling systems at the Fukushima Daiichi nuclear power plant, located just 180 miles north of Tokyo. Several explosions were recorded inside the plant. Radiation levels started to rise. Fearing a full meltdown, Japanese authorities declared an emergency.

The Japanese police have reported almost 27,000 quake-related injuries and 20,000 deaths. Additionally, 129,530 buildings were destroyed and 254,101 buildings were partially destroyed. A shocking 701,865 buildings were damaged. Hundreds of thousands of residents were evacuated. Many of these families will never see their homes again. Some do not want to go back. The ground is so contaminated with radiation that they cannot rebuild. Plus people fear that radiation has tainted the local supply of food.

Everyone around the Fukushima plant lost their homes—that's almost 100,000 people! A year after the quake, about 16,000 residents near the plant in the towns of Kawauchi and Tamura have been allowed to return to some areas within the towns (other areas are too contaminated). There is still a 12-mile zone around the plant that remains closed to everyone. Removal of contaminated material will take years. The accident has caused many in Japan to seriously consider more clean energy technologies like wind, solar, and geothermal.

The damage could have been much worse. The Japanese have very strict building codes, and residents participate in emergency warning drills. Any of the older homes that were not up to code were destroyed by the quake. The citizens of Japan are demanding even stronger codes because scientists estimate that there is up to a 70 percent chance that a magnitude 7.0 earthquake or higher will hit Tokyo in the next four years.

The tsunami was particularly destructive and accounted for over 90 percent of the deaths. Sea walls built to keep out the water were only ten feet high in Sendai City near where the quake was centered. In the rest of Japan, sea walls are often at least 30 feet high. In Miyako, one of the hardest hit cities, the tsunami reached a height of over 130 feet—that's as high as a 13-story building. In many other areas, the tsunami was over 75 feet and swept away entire towns.

In addition to the human devastation, there was a terrible economic cost felt in Japan and around the world. The economic losses are in the hundreds of billions of dollars. Rebuilding Japan's north coast will take many years. But the Japanese have many great resources that will lead them to recovery:

money for food, emergency supplies, health care workers, and engineers. They also have the infra-structure—or foundational facilities, such as roads, airports, and power plants—to send emergency crews where they are needed most.

Despite the destruction and loss of life, major earthquakes often produce startling scientific facts. For instance, the US Geological Survey estimates that the 2011 Japan earthquake moved Honshu Island nearly eight feet!

Fire trucks are seen among the debris as the firefighters were caught by the tsunami on the way to extinguish a fire caused by the earthquake.

Glossary

aftershock—a tremor (or one of a series of tremors) occurring after the main shock of an earthquake

aftershocks—smaller earthquakes after the main one

BCE—before the Common Era, replaces previously used BC (before Christ), which covers the period of history before Christ was born

capsize—to overturn

contaminated—make (something) impure by exposure to or addition of a poisonous or polluting substance

epicenter—the ground above where the earthquake starts

epicenter—the part of the Earth's surface directly above the focus of an earthquake

eyewitness—a person who sees something happen

fault—a place where two plates scrape against each other

harbor—a place where boats dock to be safe from storms

impact—to have a direct effect on

jetty, jetties—a structure extended into the sea to protect a harbor

lake bed—the ground at the bottom of a lake

magnitude—measure of the energy released during an earthquake; the great size or extent of something

Pacific Ring of Fire—a band around the Pacific Ocean where two tectonic plates (part of the Earth's crust) meet

poverty—the state of being extremely poor

priceless—too valuable to have a price

Richter Scale—a scale used to measure the strength of earthquakes

rubble—broken pieces of a building

rupture—to burst or break

sanitation—conditions relating to public health, such as providing clean drinking water or adequate sewage disposal

scorch—to burn

shock waves—energy that travels underground, but causes earthquakes at the surface

Tenochtitlán—possibly the largest city in the fourteenth-century world; built on islands in Lake Texcoco, Mexico

tremor—a small earthquake

tsunami—huge waves created by an earthquake or volcano underwater

Index